GIGANTIC DRILLING RIGS

MARIE ROGERS

PowerKiDS
press™

New York

Published in 2022 by The Rosen Publishing Group, Inc.
29 East 21st Street, New York, NY 10010

First Edition

Portions of this work were originally authored by Kenny Allen and published as *Drilling Rigs*. All new material in this edition authored by Marie Rogers.

Editor: Greg Roza
Cover Design: Michael Flynn
Interior Layout: Rachel Rising

Photo Credits: Cover, p. 1 Mr.PK/Shutterstock.com; pp. 4, 6, 8, 10, 12, 14 ,16 ,18, 20, 21 (background) 13Imagery/Shutterstock.com; p. 5 Maximov Denis/Shutterstock.com; p. 7 I am a Stranger/Shutterstock.com; p. 9 Vladimir Melnikov/Shutterstock.com; p. 11 HHakim/E+/Getty Images; p. 13 Spencer Platt/Staff/Getty Images News/Getty Images; p. 15 Bloomberg/Contributor/Getty Images; p. 16 Mettus/Shutterstock.com; p. 17 sasacvetkovic33/iStock/Getty images; p. 19 MediaNews Group/Boulder Daily Camera via Getty Images/Contributor/Getty Images; p. 21 Kuni Takahashi/Contributor/Getty Images News/Getty Images; p. 21 Sharasaur/Shutterstock.com.

Library of Congress Cataloging-in-Publication Data

Names: Rogers, Marie, 1990- author.
Title: Gigantic drilling rigs / Marie Rogers.
Description: New York : PowerKids Press, [2022] | Series: Big jobs, big
   tools! | Includes index.
Identifiers: LCCN 2020021700 | ISBN 9781725326675 (library binding) | ISBN
   9781725326651 (paperback) | ISBN 9781725326668 (6 pack)
Subjects: LCSH: Oil well drilling rigs–Juvenile literature.
Classification: LCC TN871.5 .R64 2022 | DDC 622/.33810284–dc23
LC record available at https://lccn.loc.gov/2020021700

Manufactured in the United States of America

Some of the images in this book illustrate individuals who are models. The depictions do not imply actual situations or events.

CPSIA Compliance Information: Batch #CSPK22. For Further Information contact Rosen Publishing, New York, New York at 1-800-237-9932.

Find us on

CONTENTS

Drilling Holes

Drilling rigs drill holes in the ground. Some drilling rigs are huge! The largest drilling rigs can reach many miles underground. They need hundreds of workers! Why do drilling rigs drill? Let's find out!

Deeper and Deeper

Drilling rigs make boreholes in the ground. Boreholes are needed to reach oil and natural gas. Drilling rigs are also used to reach water. The deepest borehole is in Russia. It's about 7.5 miles (12.1 km) deep!

Setting Up

People often set up drilling rigs in wild areas. Workers cut down trees and build roads for trucks. They dig a pit where the drilling rig will be set up. Workers also remove waste rock.

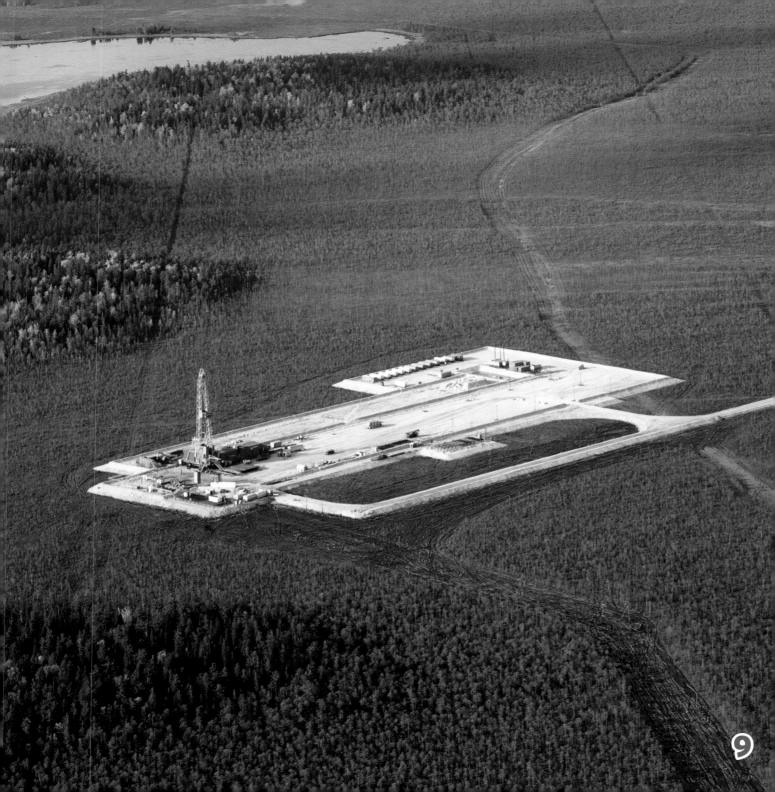

Power Up!

Drilling rigs use different kinds of **motors**. Some gas motors move parts to power the drill. Other motors make electricity. This electricity may power smaller motors. These electric motors work together to power the drill too.

Standing Tall

Drilling rigs have a tall **frame** called a derrick. The derrick holds the drill in place. It has ropes or cables that raise and lower the drill. Drilling rigs on land can be 70 feet (21.3 m) tall or more.

13

Drilling!

Now the drilling starts! The derrick lowers drill pipes into the borehole. Just one pipe can be 30 feet (9.1 m) long. When one pipe is almost all the way underground, workers **connect** a new pipe to it.

Cutting Through Rock

A drill bit is connected on the end of the drill pipe. The bit cuts through dirt and rock as the drill pipe goes lower. Some bits spin. Some pound like a hammer. Others have **blades**.

Pumps and Pits

Drilling into the ground makes a lot of waste rock and mud. These get in the way of drilling. Drilling rigs use machines called **pumps** to force rock and mud into waste pits.

Gigantic!

Drilling rigs at sea are called oil platforms. They are gigantic! Some float. Others stand on the ocean floor. The tallest oil rig is over 2,000 feet (610 m) tall. Most of that is underwater!

Oil Platforms of the World

Heaviest
Berkut
Russian Pacific Ocean
200,000 tons (181,437 mt)

Tallest
Petronius
Gulf of Mexico
2,438 feet (610 m)

Deepest
Stones
Gulf of Mexico
9,500 feet (2,900 m)

Berkut

Petronius

GLOSSARY

blade: The flat, sharp part of a tool that's used for cutting.

connect: To join two or more things together.

frame: Something that holds up or gives shape to something.

motor: A machine that produces motion or power for doing work.

pump: A device for raising, moving, or squeezing liquids or gases.

FOR MORE INFORMATION

WEBSITES

How Offshore Drilling Works

science.howstuffworks.com/environmental/energy/offshore-drilling.htm

This article at HowStuffWorks.com discusses all there is to know about oil drilling platforms.

Oil Facts

www.scienceforkidsclub.com/oil.html

Learn more about the history of oil drilling, where oil rigs are found, and how they're used.

BOOKS

Doeden, Matt. *Finding Out About Coal, Oil, and Natural Gas.* Minneapolis, MN: LernerClassroom, 2015.

Miller, Mirella S. *Oil Worker.* North Mankato, MN: The Child's World, 2015.

Publisher's note to parents and teachers: Our editors have reviewed the websites listed here to make sure they're suitable for students. However, websites may change frequently. Please note that students should always be supervised when they access the internet.

INDEX